GETTING STAF
INDESIGN

A BEGINNERS GUIDE TO CREATING
PROFESSIONAL DOCUMENTS WITH ADOBE
INDESIGN 2020

SCOTT LA COUNTE

RIDICULOUSLY
SIMPLE BOOKS

ANAHEIM, CALIFORNIA

www.RidiculouslySimpleBooks.com

Table of Contents

Introduction 6

Getting Started 7

    Quick Menu Overview...15

    Zooming 17

The Basics 19

    Your First Rectangle! 19

    Adding Text 32

    Adding Images...37

    Adding Spreads 42

    Adding Columns 44

    Using Font Styles 50

Templates and Exporting 53

    Exporting Documents 53

    Using Templates 55

Let's Practice 57

About the Author 75

Disclaimer: *Please note, while every effort has been made to ensure accuracy, this book is not endorsed by Adobe, Inc. and should be considered unofficial.*

INTRODUCTION

Adobe InDesign is arguably one of Adobe's more underappreciated programs. Many people have gotten used to creating brochures and books using Word and Pages.

If you are a professional who cares about design, then there is no greater tool for creating a document than InDesign.

This book is intended to get you started, so you can understand what all the important features are and how to use them. You'll learn how to:

- Use menus
- Change colors
- Arrange images, shapes, and text
- Create spreads
- Create columns
- Perform wraps
- Export to different file types
- And much more!

This book isn't comprehensive; the goal is to get you up and running as quickly as possible.

Note: this book is not endorsed by Adobe, Inc and should be considered unofficial.

[1]

GETTING STARTED

This chapter will cover:
- Getting Started
- Menu overview
- Zooming and navigating around InDesign

Unsurprisingly, the first thing you see is an open / new menu; to get started, click the Create New button.

Creating a new document will give you a New Document screen that asks what kind of document it is. You can choose the presets from a previously used document, or create one based on presets for Print, Web, or Mobile.

Print   Web   Mobile

Each section will have presets on top for creating a blank document, or you can select a Template below it. You can additionally select View All Presets to see more (hint: the first four are the most popular). After the document is created, you are still able to change the preset size and settings, so don't worry about selecting the wrong one if you are unsure.

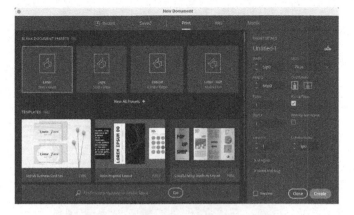

Additionally, you can use the side panel to create your own dimension. Change "Untitled-1" to whatever you want the file to be called (you can change this later). By default, Facing Pages is selected for most documents; if you are creating a single page document, make sure and deselect it. A Facing Page is when you have a layout where pages are arranged in spreads—think about a magazine or a book where you have two pages side-by-side.

PRESET DETAILS

Untitled-1

Width
66p0

Units
Picas

Height
102p0

Orientation

Pages
1

Facing Pages

Start #
1

Primary Text Frame

Columns
1

Column Gutter
1p0

> Margins

> Bleed and Slug

Preview   Close   Create

Once you have decided what you will use, select the blue Create. The document will immedi-
ately launch and will be blank unless you selected a
template.

The pink area you see helps you identify the margins; this color will not print or show up if you export it as a PDF; it is only shown in the design file. You can hide it by pressing the "W" key. Pressing it again turns it back on.

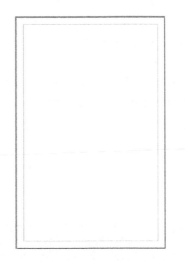

By default, the right panel will be set to "Essentials" properties. Above this panel is a dropdown to add properties for other menus. These properties menus are known in InDesign as project Workspaces.

Advanced

Book

Digital Publishing

✓ Essentials

Essentials Classic

Interactive for PDF

Printing and Proofing

Typography

Reset Essentials

New Workspace...

Delete Workspace...

Show Full Menus

In the upper left corner of the screen, you'll see a tab for the document. It's common to design multiple documents at the same time in InDesign, so tabs make it easy to have all the documents open in the same window, so you can toggle between them.

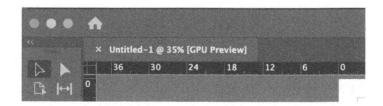

To open a second document as you work on the first, go to File > New and select the type of document.

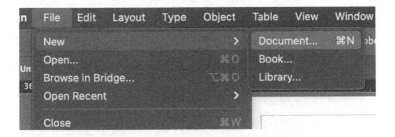

Once you select the Document type, you'll see two tabs now appear in the upper left.

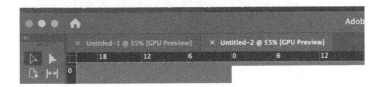

If there's something you forgot to do in your preset (you want to change the margin, for example, or switch the orientation), then go to File > Document Setup.

Document Setup

Intent: Print

Number of Pages: 1   ☑ Facing Pages

Start Page #: 1   ☐ Primary Text Frame

Page Size: Tabloid

Width: ⌃ 66p0   Orientation: ▯ ▭

Height: ⌃ 102p0

Margins

Top: ⌃ 3p0   Inside: ⌃ 3p0

Bottom: ⌃ 3p0   Outside: ⌃ 3p0

› Bleed and Slug

ⓘ Adjust page elements to   (Adjust Layout...)
document changes

☐ Preview   (Cancel)   (OK)

It's always a good idea to save your document before doing anything. Go to File > Save. It will ask for your file name and document type. The name isn't important; name it whatever you want! But the file type is important. Make sure you are saving as an InDesign file format. You will be able to export it in other formats that anyone can view (such as PDF) when you are done.

Save As

Save As: Untitled-1

Tags:

Where: Documents — iCloud

Format: InDesign 2020 document

☑ Always Save Preview Images with Documents

Cancel   Save

You can additionally go to File > Close to close the document; this is a little different than what you may be used to. It doesn't close the InDesign software—only the document.

Quick Menu Overview

The main menu you'll use in InDesign is the toolbar on the left side. There are all kinds of features there that we'll cover later. One thing you should know, however, is anytime you see a little triangle in the bottom right corner you can click your mouse and hold to bring up more options.

The document at this point looks pretty basic, but there are a lot of features buried in InDesign. If you go to Window on the top menu, you'll see what I mean. These windows represent some of the many menus and tools available to you as you work on your document.

All the menus and toolbars you see can be dragged anywhere you want on the screen; just click and hold the top of the menu and drag.

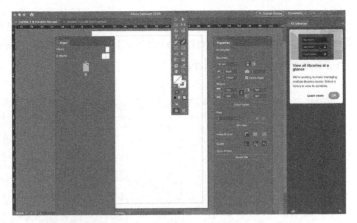

If you've dragged the windows and sort of made a mess of things, then go to Window > Workspace and Reset Essentials. This moves all the menus back to where they originally were.

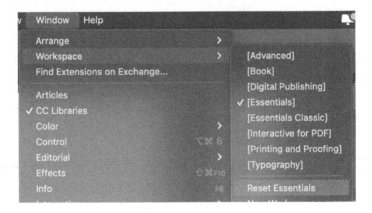

Zooming

If something is too small or you want to zoom in to make it bigger, you can either pinch and expand with your trackpad, press Command +, or use the zoom icon in your toolbar; to return to seeing everything in your window without having to scroll, click Command 0 or go to View from the top menu and Fit Page in Window.

[2]

THE BASICS

This chapter will cover:
- Understanding shapes
- Adding images and text
- Adding and understanding spreads
- Adding columns
- Using fonts

Your First Rectangle!

Rectangles don't sound very exciting, but they're a good way to learn about menus and colors.

To get started, go to the rectangle button on the left toolbar. Don't see it? That's probably because you have a different shape selected; click and hold on the shape button to see all the possible shapes, and change it back to a rectangle. You'll notice there are two rectangle icons—one has an X through it.

The icon with the X in it is to draw a dummy shape (i.e. a shape to show there will be an image there in the future, but you don't have anything for it yet).

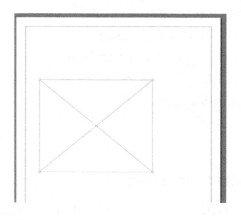

For this example, you'll want the icon below this, which draws a shape without an X in it.

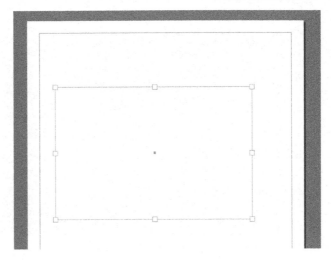

If you accidentally click outside of the box, you can select it again by using the selection icon. This icon is on the top of your left toolbar; you'll see two—the one you want is the top one (it shows an outline of an arrow, not an arrow that has a filled color).

Now that it is selected you can go to the right menu to change the appearance. You'll see all the things you can do under Appearance. To start with, let's change the Fill color; click once on the box next to Fill (it probably will be white with a red line through it).

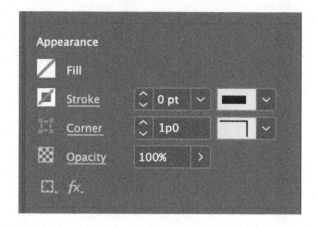

Adobe tries to make your life easier by showing you a list of common colors.

If you double click on the box with the selected color (white with a red line in the example above), you can open up the Color Picker box which has even more colors.

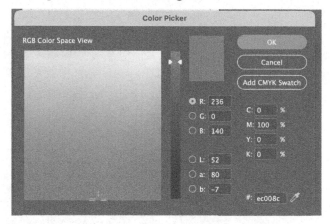

Click okay or cancel to close that box, and then click outside of the color menu box to close that box.

To create your own color, select the middle icon on the top of the color box (it looks like a painter's palette). At the bottom of this box is a rainbow and you can use the picker tool to select your color.

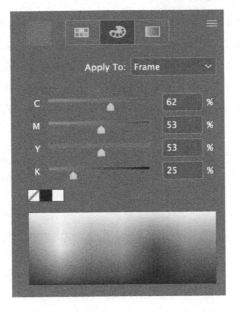

You can also click the icon in the upper right corner and select the type of colors you want to see. RGB is what's typically used because it more closely represents the color you see on your computer. If you have a color you are always using, you can select Add to Swatches and you can add the color to that first icon, which shows the popular colors. It's kind of like favoriting a color.

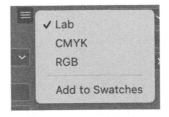

Add to Swatches is also helpful for adding branded colors; let's say you add in your company's corporate colors so you can use them in multiple documents. That's great! But when you see it in that favorite list, you'll see the color code, which isn't very friendly. You can double click that color, then unselect Name with Color Value and add in a custom color name; then you can change the name to something like "Company Blue" or whatever helps you know what the color is used for.

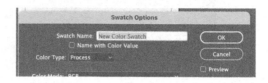

Below the Fill color is the Stroke color; this is like the border color—Fill is the inside color and Stroke is the outside. It works the same way as color fill, but you have the option next to it to choose the line weight and style.

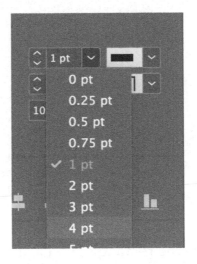

Line weight is how thick the line is.

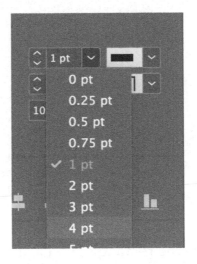

Line style lets you pick how the line looks.

I chose a size 20 wavy line in the example below.

To resize the rectangle, you'll just want to make sure it's selected, then drag those corner boxes.

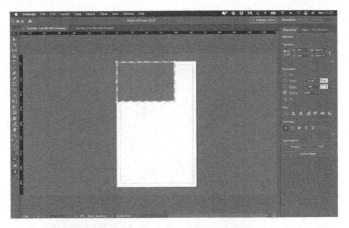

I'm dragging over the entire page so the box fills the whole document.

You can continue adding boxes over this box by using that rectangle icon again.

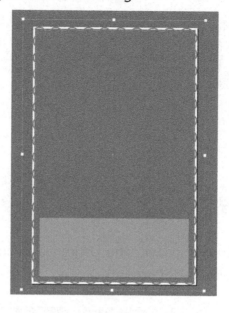

If you click on the box and hover your mouse over in the top right corner, you'll get the option to rotate an image.

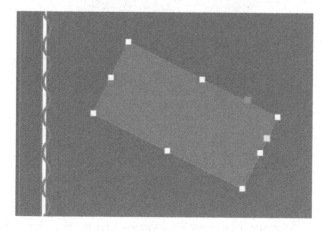

InDesign also has a helpful tool for resizing shapes; let's say you have a box, and you want to resize it to half the size. You could obviously just make the calculation yourself, but you could also go to Transform on the right menu (make sure the shape is selected) and under W (for width) or H (for height) put a "/" and add a 2. This tells InDesign that you want to resize it to half of the size; you can replace the 2 with whatever you want (e.g. a 3 for a third of the size; a 4 for a fourth of the size, etc.). You can also use the * key to times the size.

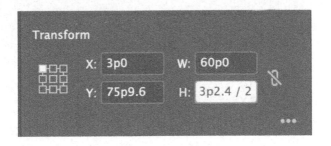

Once you have the boxes with the size that you want, you can use the arrangement to adjust how they appear. For example, let's say I want to move a box in front of another box. Just right-click the box, then click Arrange and Bring to Front.

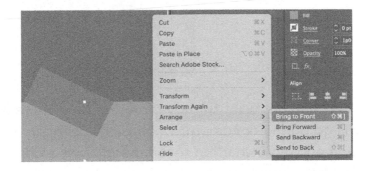

The box is now in front of the other.

Adding Text

Adding text in InDesign is done using text boxes; you've probably used text boxes before in Microsoft Word. Basically, these create boxes for the text that can be moved around—so the text isn't fixed to a specific place on the page.

To get started click the text icon on the left menu.

You might want to move the text box where it will go on the document; what many designers recommend, and what I'm recommending, is to do the text box outside of the document—just to the side of it. It's easier to work with. Once you get it to be the size and font that you want, then you can move it where you want it to go.

Once you have your box, start typing.

To change the font around, go to your right menu; the Character section has most of the tools you'll want.

The first thing in that section is the fonts that you have on your computer.

If you are in this box, you can click Find More up top, and it will show you fonts that Adobe has created. There are a lot to pick from. If you don't see this list, then you probably don't have Internet access, as they aren't installed locally on your computer.

Fonts	Find More		
Filters: ▼ ★ ⏰ ↻		Selected Text ⌄ ᴀ **A** A	
◎ Activate Adobe Fonts instantly			
› Aaux Next (18)		This is a Test	☁
› Abadi MT Pro (14)		This is a Test	☁
Abigail		This is a Test	☁
› Abolition (4)		THIS IS A TEST	☁
› Abril Display (10)		This is a Test	☁
› Abril Fatface (2)		This is a Test	☁
› Abril Text (10)		This is a Test	☁
› Abril Titling (8)		This is a Test	☁

Below font is where you can apply the font style—if you want it Bold, for example.

Next is font size.

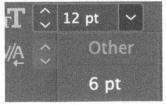

Followed by line spacing.

Paragraph is where you can adjust the alignment; if you want it center aligned, for example.

Changing the font color is similar to how you changed the box color in the last section. Double click the T icon, then pick your color.

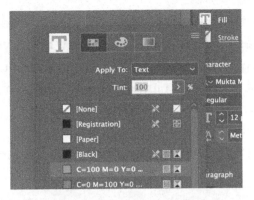

Because this is a text box, you can also give the box itself a color (it's transparent by default). To do that, click the dropdown next to Apply To and select Frame. If Frame is greyed out, that means you are currently selecting the text and you need to select the box itself. Go to the selector icon and click the box.

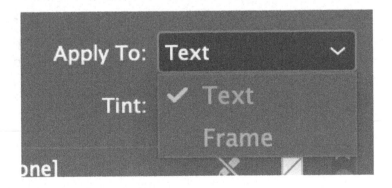

Adding Images

Next let's learn some fun stuff: adding images to your document. Before going further, you'll obviously need an image.

For the purpose of this tutorial, it doesn't matter where the image comes from, but if you will be creating any documents for commercial use, it's important you get an image that you either own the rights to or is licensed for you to use.

Once you have an image that you are ready to use, go to the right panel and click Import File.

Once you select the file, it will show a thumbnail that you can drag where you want it to go. As with text, it's easier to move it to the side of the document to get it ready. As you move it, there are two ways you can drop the image; one is a single click, which is usually not recommended—this will drop the full-size image; the second way is to drag and hold, and make a box approximately how large you want the image to be.

Let go once it's to the side that you want, and you'll see the image.

If you want to resize the image, you don't do it like you typically do on photos. You are probably used to going to the corner and dragging in to resize; if you did that, it would do a crop of sorts—the image size would stay the same but the container box would get smaller. To resize the entire image, you need to hold a shortcut key as you drag it in or out; if you are on a Mac, you hold Command+Shift; if you are on a Windows PC it's CTRL+Shift.

If you try to move the photo, make sure you are not clicking on the center where you'll see a little round button known as the content grabber—this moves the image within the container box but does not move the actual image box.

Once you are ready, click anywhere but the center to move the image where you want it to go, then adjust the size to fit in your document.

Once you have it where you want it to go, you can go to Object > Transform from the top menu to perform additional adjustments (such as flipping the image).

Object	Table	View	Window	Help	
Transform			>	Move...	⇧⌘M
Transform Again			>	Scale...	
Arrange			>	Rotate...	
Select			>	Shear...	
Group		⌘G		Rotate 90° CW	
Ungroup		⇧⌘G		Rotate 90° CCW	
Lock		⌘L		Rotate 180°	
Unlock All on Spread		⌥⌘L			
Hide		⌘3		Flip Horizontal	
Show All on Spread		⌥⌘3		Flip Vertical	
Insert HTML...				Clear Transformations	

If you decide you want a different image, then click the image, go to Quick Actions on the right side menu, and then select Import File. This will replace the image with whatever you select. You probably will have to make some adjustments if it's a different size, but the frame will be the correct size.

Quick Actions

Convert Shape	Arrange
Import File	Embed
Edit With	Reveal in Finder
Find Similar Images	

Adding Spreads

Now that you are starting to get the hang of where things are and how to add them, it's time to think about adding more pages.

InDesign will do a single page, but because most people use it for some kind of publishing (from brochures and fliers to magazines and books), you don't always add pages the same way you would in something like Word. InDesign is meant to be designed in a way where you will print something that can be folded—think about magazines: there are two side-by-side pages that are folded over; or brochures: there's often a piece of paper that is folded in threes.

So as you start designing more complex designs, adding spreads (instead of pages) is something that you will do a lot. A spread lets you add text and graphics across multiple pages.

Adding pages is easy in InDesign, but it's a manual process; you have to tell InDesign how many pages you want (and you can continue to change it as your document gets longer). To add pages, go to the right panel and change the 1 (it's to the right side of W:) to the number of pages you want. If you wanted single pages, then uncheck Facing Pages. You can also change the orientation of the pages above this.

You can zoom out to see all your pages, but when you start working with documents that have dozens of pages, this can be a little cumbersome; to see pages more quickly, click the Pages tab in the right panel. This shows your document in an outline view to help you quickly jump to the right section.

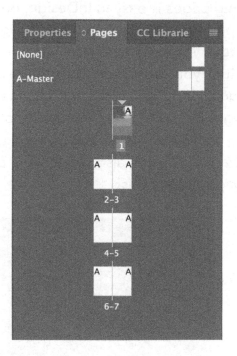

Adding Columns

As you start adding text to a document, you'll probably want to use columns. To create columns, you create text boxes just like you would for adding any normal text, but then you do something known as linking text boxes. It sounds a little complicated. It's not. It's super easy!

If you are adding text for a magazine, then chances are you already have text; you can either copy and paste it into a text box, or you can import the text using the Import File button on the right properties panel (under Quick Actions).

Once you add your text box and add content, click the red box with the plus sign in the lower right corner one time (do not click and hold).

m.zvxmn,.
m.zvxmn,.
m.zvxmn,.
m.zvxmn,.
m.zvxmn,.
m.zvxmn,.
m.zvxmn,.

Next, move the arrow where you want the text to go.

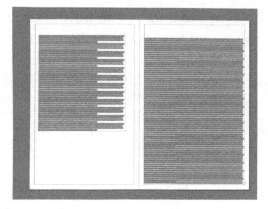

The text boxes are now linked. If you adjust one, it changes the text placement in the other automatically. You can add as many text boxes as you'd like, and adjust the sizes accordingly—yo can make them straight columns or any sizes you want (one text box can be a completely different size from the other).

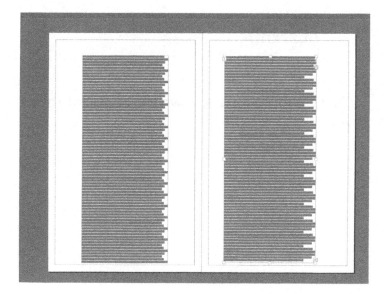

You can even add the text box to another page (which is obviously helpful if you are working on something longer—like an article that spans several pages), and it stays linked! If you delete a text box, it automatically reflows into the previous text box—it doesn't delete the text.

There's a quicker way to create columns if each column will be an equal size; click the text box with the black arrow, then go to the lower right property panel to Text Frame.

Change the 1 to the number of columns you want, then use the box to the right of this to change the gutter space (i.e. the space between the columns).

The text box selected is now two columns, but it's still linked to the other text box.

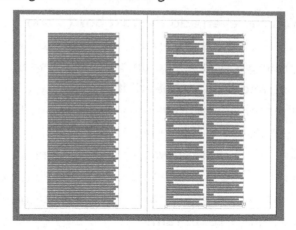

Right below the Text Frame, is the option to change your text box to a shape; click the Convert to Shape button, and select the shape you want the text to be.

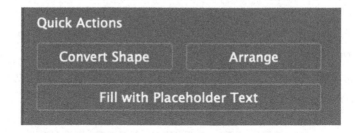

The text is now a shape!

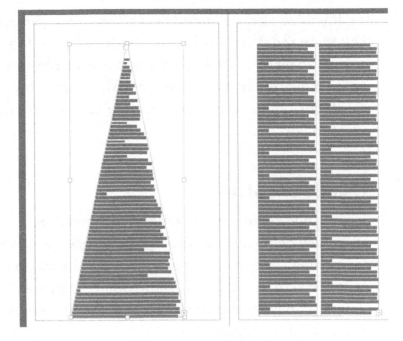

You can do this to columns as well.

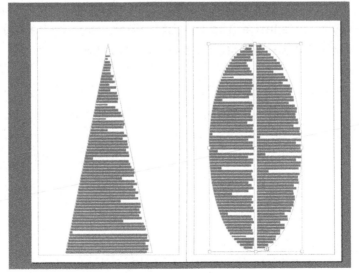

If you've already added text boxes, you can also link them together; to do this, click the box in the corner again (it's red if there's text not visible and white if everything fits in the box), then press the CTRL or Command button and drag to the box you want to link.

Using Font Styles

As your document becomes more complex, styles will help you. You can create a style for chapter or magazine titles, for example; another style for normal text; a style for subheadings; this way you don't have to reformat the text each time you add text of that style.

To add a style, first create the style one time; in the example below, I created a text box for a title style—it's large and bright. When you are happy with the appearance of the text, highlight it.

Next go to Window > Styles > Paragraph Styles.

| View | Window | Help | | | | | |

Arrange
Workspace
Find Extensions on Exchange...

Articles
CC Libraries
Color
Control
Editorial
Effects
Info
Interactive
Layers
Learn
Links
Object & Layout
Output
Overlays
Pages
PDF Comments
✓ Properties
Stroke
Styles
Text Wrap
✓ Tools
Type & Tables
Utilities

Cell Styles
Character Styles
Object Styles
Paragraph Styles
Table Styles

This brings up a style window. In the bottom lower right corner, click the icon of the square with the + sign.

Next, name the style—it can be whatever you want.

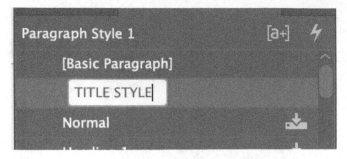

Anytime you want to use this style, highlight the text, go to Window > Styles > Paragraph Styles, and click the style name.

[3]
TEMPLATES AND EXPORTING

Exporting Documents

Through this book, you've been using an InDesign project file. That means you can share the file with someone and they can open it in InDesign; if they don't have InDesign, however, they won't be able to see it. When you get to the stage where you want to share it, you need to export it as a different file type.

To export, go to File > Export.

File	Edit	Layout	Type	Object
New				>
Open...				⌘ O
Browse in Bridge...				⌥⌘ O
Open Recent				>
Close				⌘ W
Save				⌘ S
Save As...				⇧⌘ S
Check In...				
Save a Copy...				⌥⌘ S
Revert				
Search Adobe Stock...				
Place...				⌘ D
Place from CC Libraries...				
Import XML...				
Import PDF Comments...				
Adobe PDF Presets				>
Export...				⌘ E

There are lots of different file types. PDF is the most popular and the most universal, but it really depends on the type of project you are working on; if this is an eBook, for example, then you'd probably want to export it as an ePub (hint: you'll notice there are two types of ePubs: Fixed and Reflowable—Fixed means it retains more of the look / feel of the document, which is good for things like textbooks; Reflowable is more suitable for eReaders).

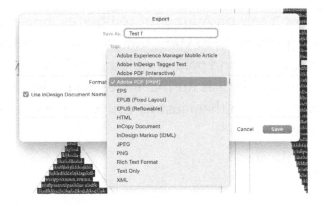

Using Templates

Templates are a great way to create a document quickly. Adobe has templates for everything from social media posts to eBooks. These templates will create a dummy file with a style already created; all you have to do is add the content and update any text.

Don't rely on Adobe for templates, however; it's a good place to start, but you can find thousands of free and paid templates online. You would download these as normal InDesign project files, and then open them just as you would a saved document.

[4]
LET'S PRACTICE

As a way of recapping what we've learned, let's create a new document: letter size. We are going to create a short biography about Mark Twain. I'm going to grab a few license free photo of Twain off Wikipedia, and also get license free images of the Mississippi River to go with the document.

If you recall, to add an image quickly, go to Import File on the right side, then find your image.

I'm going to turn the image into a shape (you can do this by selecting the image with the black arrow, and then selecting the shape under Convert Shape under quick actions).

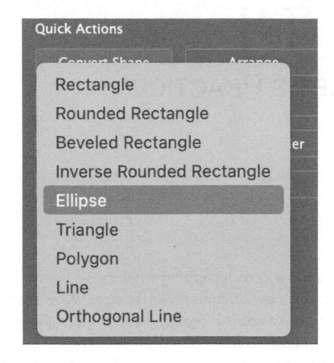

I now have my image as a circle.

Next, I'm going to create a background color. I'm going to create a box over the entire page, pick my color on the right side, then right click and do Arrange and Send to Back.

Cut	⌘X
Copy	⌘C
Paste	⌘V
Paste in Place	⌥⇧⌘V
Search Adobe Stock...	
Zoom	>
Transform	>
Transform Again	>
Arrange	>
Select	>
Lock	⌘L

Arrange submenu:
| Send Backward | ⌘[|
| Send to Back | ⇧⌘[|

I'm going to create another box that's half the size of the main box. To do this, I copy and paste the box, change the color, then go to Transform on the right and do "/2" in the height field.

Transform panel:

Transform

X: 0p0.771   W: 51p0

Y: 0p0   H: 66p0/2

I'm not happy with how it looks as a circle, so I'm going to click the image and change it back to a rectangle (Convert to Shape and Rectangle).

If the image looks off, then right click and do Fitting > Fill Frame Proportionally.

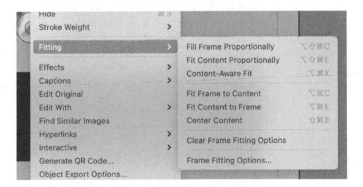

Next, I'll move the black top up above and adjust it a little; I'll put the article title up there.

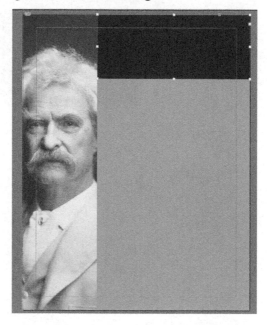

Next I'll create some text for the title, making sure to change the font color.

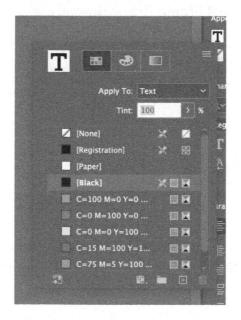

I'll also change the font size...

And the actual font.

I created two text boxes; one that's large and has the article title, and one that's smaller with the author name.

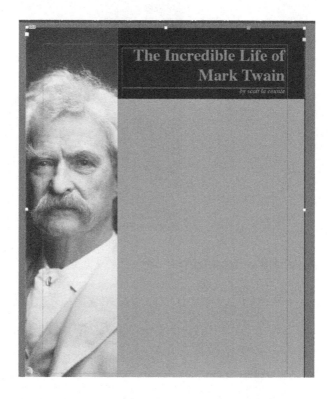

Next, I want to create the content for the article. I have it already, so I'll just go into Word and copy and paste it into InDesign. You'll see there's a red box on the bottom with a + sign; that means the content doesn't fit in the text box, which is fine because we are spreading it across several pages.

I resized the box to fit the entire page.

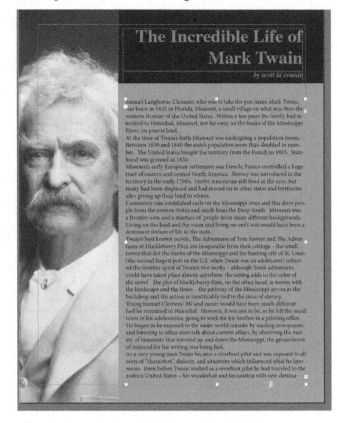

This looks good so far, but it still doesn't fit on the page, so I need to create additional pages. I'll create two more (using the right properties panel and changing the 1 to 3).

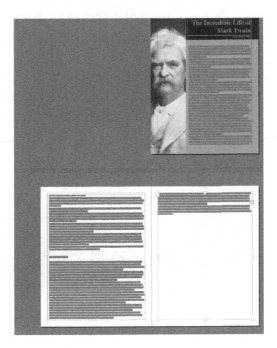

Next, I'll click that red box on the text box, and I'll drag it to the second page, then repeat and drag it to the third page. So I have three linked text boxes.

Next, I'll turn the frame to a box with two columns.

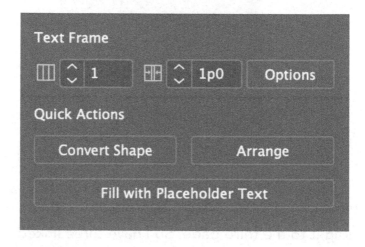

I want to put a Mark Twain quote in the article, and have it float in line with the text; this is pretty simple to do—and it works with both text boxes and images.

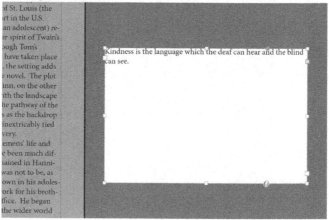

Drag the text box where you want it to wrap, then go to Window > Text Wrap.

Next, select the type of wrapping you want.

I rotated the box slightly; notice how it's now wrapped in the sample below?

Now let's go to the next page and put in an image of the Mississippi River that spans across two pages. Right now, it's in front of the text, which is fine. Just right click it and send it behind the text.

Next, I'm going to give each of the text boxes a white background, but change their transparency so you can see through the background; click on Opacity as you click the text box.

Appearance

Fill

Stroke

Corner   1p0

Opacity   70%   >

fx.

Now you can make out the image behind the text boxes.

I want to add in an image to this page; instead of inserting the image, however, I'm just going to create a shape that represents the image, then wrap it around the text.

In the image below, you can see that there's now a white shape to represent where an image will go.

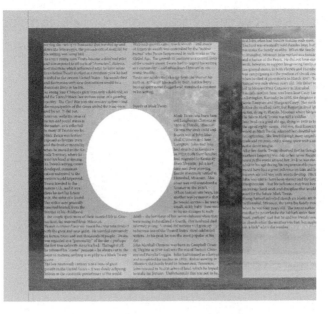

Once I have my image, I just drag it into that white shape. It's a little easier to manage when you do it with this method.

You are now ready to export your design and share the creation with the world!

ABOUT THE AUTHOR

Scott La Counte is a librarian and writer. His first book, *Quiet, Please: Dispatches from a Public Librarian* (Da Capo 2008) was the editor's choice for the Chicago Tribune and a Discovery title for the Los Angeles Times; in 2011, he published the YA book The N00b Warriors, which became a #1 Amazon bestseller; his most recent book is *Jesus Ascended. What Does That Mean?*

He has written dozens of best-selling how-to guides on tech products.

You can connect with him at ScottDouglas.org.

Made in the USA
Las Vegas, NV
20 January 2021